WORK SMARTER NOT HARDER

The *SERVICE THAT SELLS!* Workbook

Alcohol Beverage Service

PENCOM
INTERNATIONAL

ISBN #1-879239-18-3

PUB-549/1998

Contents

Let's Get Started 1
How to Use this Workbook 1

Maximize Your Opportunities 3
How Much More? 3

Section One: Product Knowledge 4
Need To Know 4
Nice To Know 5
    Alcohol Beverage Guide 6
Less Is More 26
    Role Play 26
Action Plan 26

Section Two: Caring Behavior 27
Little Something Extras 27
Personalize Your Service 29
Watch Your Language 29
Talk the Talk 30
Say You're Sorry 30
Stroke Your Customers 30
Pay Attention 30
    Role Play 31
Add Some Flair 31
    Role Play 31
Action Plan 32

Section Three: Precision Service 33
Stay Out of the Weeds 33
Drive I-135 34
The Perfect Pour 35
Opening Wine 37
    Role Play 38
That's the Spirit 38
Action Plan 38

Section Four: Sales Performance 39
Prop Up Your Sales 39
Recommend the Larger Size 40
Break It Down 40
    Role Play 41
Get to the Point 41
Assume the Sale 41
Five Times To Sell Wine 42
Catch the Spirit 44
    Role Play 45
Go for Two 45
    Role Play 46
The Parade 46
Action Plan 46

Final Action Plan 47
And One Last Thing 50
Pencom International Products 51

Let's Get Started

Work Smarter, Not Harder! The Service That Sells! Workbook for Alcohol Beverage Service has the potential to improve your service delivery and earning power like no other training tool you've used. Whether you're tending bar or serving drinks out on the floor, you'll be primed for success once you master the strategies presented in the following pages.

To read *The Service That Sells! Workbook for Alcohol Beverage Service* is only part of what it takes to reap the rewards. It's also important to complete the "Put It on Paper" and "It's Your Turn" exercises to the best of your ability, then use role plays — preferably with a manager or trainer — to practice what you've learned.

At that point, you'll be ready to apply what you've practiced during your very next shift. Why put it off? As a result of your efforts, you'll be able to:

- **Provide better service**
- **Increase your sales**
- **Earn bigger tips**
- **Have more fun at work**

The Service That Sells! Workbook for Alcohol Beverage Service is the companion of *The Service That Sells! Workbook for Foodservice.* They're powerful in tandem, although either can be completed without the other.

How to Use this Workbook

The Service That Sells! Workbook for Alcohol Beverage Service is not about sneaky tricks of the trade. It *is* about giving guests what they want in a way that enhances their perception of what they've received.

The contents are divided into three key sections — *Caring Behavior, Precision Service* and *Sales Performance* — each inherently connected, each representing an area of opportunity to wow guests with your service delivery and pump up your sales of beer, wine and spirits.

Think of these sections as a "three-legged stool." Without each leg in place, the stool can't stand on its own. It's impossible, for example, to deliver *Precision Service* and *Sales Performance* if your *Caring Behavior* comes up short.

The glue holding the three-legged stool together is *Product Knowledge*. You can't sell and serve what you don't know. In fact, you'll be fine-tuning your knowledge of the bar before delving into the three legs of *Service That Sells!*

While it's possible to finish the entire workbook in one sitting, it's better to spread it out over four or five days, spending the time to read the introductory material and tackle one section at a time. Ask your manager what time line he or she wants you to follow.

 Be sure to fill out the Action Step at the end of each section. You'll be asked to transfer the best ideas to a Final Action Plan, which will serve as a daily reminder of how you're going to get the most out of completing *Work Smarter, Not Harder! The Service That Sells! Workbook for Alcohol Beverage Service*

Maximize Your Opportunities

If you remember nothing else from this workbook, keep in mind that in every sales opportunity, there's a service opportunity, and in every service opportunity, there's a sales opportunity. Checking to see how guests are enjoying their cocktails is your *service* opportunity. Suggesting a second round is your *sales* opportunity.

Guests are on your side. They want to have a good time. Suggesting food and beverage items they'd like — "soft selling" — results in better service and more tips.

How Much More?

Let's distinguish the service-oriented salesperson from the order-taker, each serving a four-top:

Order-Taker's Tab		Salesperson's Tab	
1 gin/tonic	3.00	1 Beefeater/tonic	3.75
2 draft beers (small)	5.00	2 Coors Light (large)	6.00
1 water	.00	1 flavored iced tea	1.50
0 appetizers	.00	1 nachos	4.95
Total	$8.00	Total	$16.20
15% Tip	$1.20	**15% Tip**	**$2.43**

The bottom line — a $2.43 tip for the salesperson, only $1.20 for the order-taker, a difference of more than a dollar. A buck may not sound like much, but over time it can really add up.

Put it on PAPER

Think about how many guests you serve in an average shift, then multiply that figure by the number of days you work per week, per month, per year. How much extra in tips could you take home by increasing your per-person check average by just $1?

Let's find out.

$1.00 x _____ x _____ x %15 (tip) = _____
              Guests served in a shift   shifts per week

$1.00 x _____ x _____ x %15 (tip) = _____
              Guests served in a shift   shifts per month

$1.00 x _____ x _____ x %15 (tip) = _____
              Guests served in a shift   shifts per year

If you want a guaranteed pay raise, you don't have to see your manager. Just improve your sales and customer service. This *Service That Sells! Workbook for Alcohol Beverage Service* will show you how.

Section One: Product Knowledge

Before diving into *Caring Behavior, Precision Service* and *Sales Performance* — the three-legged stool of *Service That Sells!* — it's essential to fine-tune your product knowledge.

You know, of course, the importance of knowing your products inside and out. If you can't describe what's available in a meaningful way, you're doing a disservice to your operation and the guests it attracts.

How much product knowledge will get the job done? Let's keep it simple, dividing what you should know into "Need To Know" and "Nice To Know."

Need To Know

Whether you're a newcomer to your operation or a seasoned pro, you should know enough about your selection of beers, wines and spirits to be able to:

- Recommend your favorites or the most popular brands.
- Recite prices.
- Describe presentation, including serving size, glassware and type of garnish.
- Point out basic distinguishing characteristics.

Beer, for example, generally falls into two categories: ales and lagers.

Ales use top-fermenting yeast, which means the brewing magic takes place at the top of the fermenting tank. They often have a fruity aroma and a complex, robust flavor.

Lagers, which tend to be bottom-fermented, are usually more bubbly and less bitter than their ale counterparts. They're smooth and refreshing, at their best when served ice-cold.

Wine generally falls into three categories: red, white and blush. After deciding on a color, guests will become interested in taste, which is best described using a scale between dry and sweet.

Dry wines, which have a relatively low sugar content, go well with robust fare — steaks and chops, for example — and food with heavy sauces.

Sweet wines, on the other hand, suit fish dishes, salads, and foods with light sauces. Rules of thumb, however, are meant to be broken. Give guests what they want.

Spirits generally fall into three categories: well, premium and super-premium. The main thing you need to remember is that premium and super-premium drinks taste better than their well counterparts, usually because of quality differences in ingredients or in the distillation process.

Suggest premium drinks first, then walk guests up the ladder if they show interest in super-premium selections.

Nice To Know

Now that you understand what you *need to know* about beer, wine and spirits, it's time to mix in some *nice to know*. Consider it "product wisdom" — the kind of wisdom that raises guests' interest in the products you're selling while enhancing the perceived level of your service professionalism.

Guests are becoming more and more interested in the story behind the story. They want to know what makes a particular craft beer pleasingly bitter, why the wine they're drinking is so mellow, what gives their whiskey a smoky flavor. These are defining moments separating "product knowledge" from "product wisdom."

- With knowledge, you can inform guests about the price, size and general taste of a product.
- With wisdom, you can recite fun facts that dazzle guests and promote sales all the more.

Perhaps the beer's flavorful hops come from the Yakima Valley in Washington. It might be a third-generation wine maker who shapes the Merlot's fruity nuances. Maybe the vodka is distilled four times, which produces an unparalleled smoothness.

Collect as much product wisdom as you can, memorizing special characteristics that are easy to remember and set one brand apart from another.

Alcohol Beverage Guide

To build your bank of product knowledge and product wisdom — your ticket to improved service, higher sales and bigger tips — complete the Alcohol Beverage Guide beginning on the next page and refer back to it whenever you want to infuse some zip into your sales dialogue.

The beer, wine and spirits listed are top sellers, longtime favorites or rising stars in the marketplace. As a resource for you, pertinent product knowledge and product wisdom have been provided for each brand. Ultimately, put the information into your own words, forming dialogue that appeals to the guests you serve.

In the two spaces marked "Other Brand" under each category, fill in additional selections you could recommend to guests, including some product knowledge and product wisdom of your own. To get that information, you may need to consult with your bar manager. Product labels and the Internet are other good sources.

CRAFT BEER

Brand: Samuel Adams Boston Lager

Product Knowledge: A malty, slightly sweet lager with a spicy, hoppy undertone.

Product Wisdom: The rich amber color comes from two-row summer barley, with a note of crystal malt.

Brand: Pete's Wicked Ale

Product Knowledge: The blend of pale, caramel and chocolate malts, along with Brewer's Gold hops, yields a satisfying, full-flavored brew.

Product Wisdom: The original American brown ale.

Brand: Full Sail Amber Ale

Product Knowledge: A rich, full-bodied ale that finishes with a tang of spicy floral hops.

Product Wisdom: An Oregon brewery, Full Sail has resisted contract brewing, computerization and technology in favor of making their brews by hand using traditional methods.

Other Brand:

Product Knowledge:

Product Wisdom:

Other Brand:

Product Knowledge:

Product Wisdom:

DOMESTIC BEER

Brand: Coors Light

Product Knowledge: Known as "The Silver Bullet," a premium light beer with just 144 calories per 12-ounce serving.

Product Wisdom: Brewed in Golden, Colo., it's Coors' largest selling brand and the fourth largest in the United States.

Brand: Budweiser

Product Knowledge: A classic American lager with a clean, crisp taste.

Product Wisdom: Budweiser is the only major beer in the world using the traditional beechwood aging process to age and naturally carbonate the product.

Brand: Miller Genuine Draft

Product Knowledge: Cold-filtered to produce a smooth, highly drinkable beer.

Product Wisdom: Miller doesn't hire actors for its MGD television ads, preferring to feature real people doing their thing.

Other Brand:

Product Knowledge:

Product Wisdom:

Other Brand:

Product Knowledge:

Product Wisdom:

IMPORT BEER

Brand: Heineken

Product Knowledge: An import from Holland with a clean, pleasantly bitter character.

Product Wisdom: The world's most popular import beer.

Brand: Corona Extra

Product Knowledge: Smooth and refreshing, often served with a lime.

Product Wisdom: The No. 1 import beer from Mexico, and No. 2 import in the world.

Brand: Guinness Stout

Product Knowledge: Known for its thick, creamy foam head and deep, black body.

Product Wisdom: Traditionally brewed in Dublin, Ireland, for more than 230 years.

Other Brand:

Product Knowledge:

Product Wisdom:

Other Brand:

Product Knowledge:

Product Wisdom:

RED WINE (Merlot)

Brand: Sutter Home (1996)

Product Knowledge: Medium-bodied with the aromas of cherries and herbal spice, and the rich, juicy flavors of cherries and plums.

Product Wisdom: Six months' aging in French and American oak softens and rounds out this Merlot, making it entirely drinkable upon release.

Brand: Kendall-Jackson Vintner's Reserve (1996)

Product Knowledge: A fruity wine with distinct berry and plum aromas.

Product Wisdom: Its grapes are grown on the hillside vineyards of California's North Coast, which produces its unique flavors.

Brand: Smith & Hook (1995)

Product Knowledge: Pronounced vanilla and black raspberry aromas, followed by cinnamon and cherry flavors.

Product Wisdom: Produced at a family owned and operated winery located in the Santa Lucia Highlands high above John Steinbeck's beloved Salinas Valley.

Other Brand:

Product Knowledge:

Product Wisdom:

Other Brand:

Product Knowledge:

Product Wisdom:

RED WINE (Cabernet Sauvignon)

Brand: Turning Leaf Sonoma Reserve (1994)

Product Knowledge: A complex California wine with flavors of blackberry, cassis and black pepper.

Product Wisdom: Aged for a minimum of nine months, which imparts its pleasing complexity.

Brand: Talus (1995)

Product Knowledge: A flavorful California wine, not as heavy and dry like some Cabernet Sauvignon.

Product Wisdom: Centuries ago winemakers terraced hillsides in preparation for planting. "Talus," which literally means man-made hillside, refers to this ancient practice.

Brand: Robert Mondavi (1995)

Product Knowledge: This Napa Valley wine is known for its velvety layers of cassis, ripe berry, plum and spice.

Product Wisdom: Aged in small French oak barrels and bottled without filtration, which adds to its complexity.

Other Brand:

Product Knowledge:

Product Wisdom:

Other Brand:

Product Knowledge:

Product Wisdom:

WHITE WINE (Chardonnay)

Brand: Clos Du Bois (1997)

Product Knowledge: An elegant, mellow Sonoma County wine that suits a variety of dishes, especially poultry, light pastas and salads.

Product Wisdom: Fermented in French oak barrels in a costly, handmade process which yields a Chardonnay of richness, balance and great varietal character.

Brand: Columbia Crest Valley Estate Series (1995)

Product Knowledge: Silky smooth, layered with nutmeg, nectarine and apple flavors.

Product Wisdom: Crafted from classic European grapes grown on the Estate Vineyards in the Columbia Valley in Washington.

Brand: Meridian (1996)

Product Knowledge: A rich, complex white with a lush varietal character.

Product Wisdom: The lushness comes from the rolling hills, cool ocean breezes and well-drained soils of the Santa Barbara Coast, where the grapes are grown.

Other Brand:

Product Knowledge:

Product Wisdom:

Other Brand:

Product Knowledge:

Product Wisdom:

WHITE WINE (Sauvignon Blanc)

Brand: Buena Vista (1997)

Product Knowledge: Gold-medal-winning wine packed with aromas and flavors of pears, peaches, citrus and tropical fruit.

Product Wisdom: The majority of wine is from the renown Lake County Vineyards, complemented by carefully chosen lots throughout California.

Brand: Fetzer Echo Ridge (1996)

Product Knowledge: Its crisp, bright finish ideally suits herb-roasted chicken dishes, seafood and salads.

Product Wisdom: Echo Ridge is a beautiful vista overlooking a meandering creekbed in Mendocina County, Calif.

Brand: Rodney Strong Charlotte's Home (1997)

Product Knowledge: Richly textured with passion fruit, fig and lemon-lime flavors.

Product Wisdom: The acidity produces the refreshing quality of this white wine, balanced with a bright mineral and spice component.

Other Brand:

Product Knowledge:

Product Wisdom:

Other Brand:

Product Knowledge:

Product Wisdom:

BLUSH WINE

Brand: Sutter Home (1997)

Product Knowledge: The original White Zinfandel, with berrylike aromas and crisp, delicately fruity flavors.

Product Wisdom: Established in 1890, Sutter Home has been owned since 1947 by the Trinchero Family, who has a long tradition of premium winemaking.

Brand: Beringer (1997)

Product Knowledge: Soft and blush-colored, preserving the fresh berry flavors and aromas of the Zinfandel grape.

Product Wisdom: Beringer has been producing quality wines since 1876, more than 120 years.

Brand: Vandange Autumn Harvest

Product Knowledge: Sweet and tangy, with pleasant aromas of cranberry and raspberry.

Product Wisdom: The grape harvest, a time of anticipation and excitement, is known as Vandange (Von-donj) in French.

Other Brand:

Product Knowledge:

Product Wisdom:

Other Brand:

Product Knowledge:

Product Wisdom:

AMERICAN WHISKEY

Brand: Maker's Mark

Product Knowledge: Flavorful and smooth, not as pungent as a lot of bourbons. Made with pure limestone spring water and wheat instead of rye.

Product Wisdom: The only handmade bourbon in the world, and the only distillery in America to rotate its barrels during the aging process, which ensures product consistency.

Brand: Jack Daniel's

Product Knowledge: A full-flavored Tennessee sour mash whiskey.

Product Wisdom: Produced at the oldest registered distillery in the United States — seven generations of tradition.

Brand: Jim Beam

Product Knowledge: Everything you expect from a Kentucky straight bourbon whiskey.

Product Wisdom: Originated by Jacob Beam in 1795, more than 200 years ago.

Other Brand:

Product Knowledge:

Product Wisdom:

Other Brand:

Product Knowledge:

Product Wisdom:

CANADIAN WHISKY

Brand: Canadian Club Classic

Product Knowledge: Aged 12 years to produce a rich, robust whisky.

Product Wisdom: Drained from the barrels after maturation, blended a second time, then returned to cask, ensuring a smooth, mellow bouquet and flavor.

Brand: Crown Royal

Product Knowledge: Superbly light and mellow.

Product Wisdom: Originally created as a gift for Britain's King George and his queen to commemorate their visit to Canada in 1939.

Brand: Canadian Mist

Product Knowledge: Known for its mellow character and excellent bouquet.

Product Wisdom: The rareness of the Canadian whiskies blended produces the pleasing smoothness of the end product.

Other Brand:

Product Knowledge:

Product Wisdom:

Other Brand:

Product Knowledge:

Product Wisdom:

BLENDED SCOTCH WHISKY

Brand: Cutty Sark

Product Knowledge: Easy-drinking blend using more than 30 of the highest quality malt whiskies.

Product Wisdom: Aged in oak casks and "married" for another six months to deliver a consistent taste.

Brand: Dewar's "White Label"

Product Knowledge: Sweet, faintly spicy and malty, a luscious blend.

Product Wisdom: There is no recipe for Dewar's. The secret to blending lies in the Master Blender's nose.

Brand: Chivas Regal

Product Knowledge: Distinguished by its light, lingering aroma, full, smooth palate and balanced flavor with a hint of smoke.

Product Wisdom: Known as "Scotland's Prince of Whiskies."

Other Brand:

Product Knowledge:

Product Wisdom:

Other Brand:

Product Knowledge:

Product Wisdom:

SINGLE-MALT SCOTCH WHISKY

Brand: Glendronach 15 Y.O.

Product Knowledge: Aged in sherry casks producing a sweet, not-so-harsh taste. Ideal for "starter" single-malt drinkers.

Product Wisdom: The only 15 Y.O. malt aged completely in sherry casks available in the United States and one of only two "sherry" malts in the world.

Brand: The Glenrothes

Product Knowledge: A natural malt, using no additives or colors, with a smooth, well-balanced taste.

Product Wisdom: One of the finest single malts of Speyside, long regarded as the premium single-malt-producing area of Scotland.

Brand: Laphroaig 15 Y.O.

Product Knowledge: A smoky, peaty, very challenging malt whisky. Not for the weak of spirit.

Product Wisdom: A product of the Islay region in Scotland, known for its heavy, full-bodied whiskies.

Other Brand:

Product Knowledge:

Product Wisdom:

Other Brand:

Product Knowledge:

Product Wisdom:

IRISH WHISKEY

Brand: Tullamore Dew

Product Knowledge: Smoother and lighter than other Irish whiskies, great tasting and easy drinking.

Product Wisdom: Triple-distilled, then matured slowly in oak casts to develop the rich, mellow taste.

Brand: Jameson

Product Knowledge: Triple-distilled from the finest Irish barley, producing distinctive, smooth characteristics.

Product Wisdom: The best-selling Irish whiskey around the world.

Brand: Bushmills

Product Knowledge: Blenders marry a single malt whiskey to a single grain whiskey to create the premium spirit.

Product Wisdom: Produced at the world's oldest distillery, which began operations in 1608.

Other Brand:

Product Knowledge:

Product Wisdom:

Other Brand:

Product Knowledge:

Product Wisdom:

GIN

Brand: Beefeater

Product Knowledge: Infused with the wild flavor of juniper, the subtle sweetness of angelica and the spicy orange of coriander.

Product Wisdom: Beefeater represents the corps of men William the Conqueror hand-picked almost 1,000 years ago to guard the tower of London.

Brand: Tanqueray

Product Knowledge: A well-rounded London gin and the brand of choice for James Bond.

Product Wisdom: The pineapple emblem on the bottle is an integral part of the Tanqueray family crest as well as a traditional symbol of hospitality.

Brand: Bombay

Product Knowledge: Subtle yet full-flavored, another distinctive London gin.

Product Wisdom: Produced in a unique distillation process whereby vapor passes through racks of selected natural flavoring agents, including coriander, liquorice, lemon peel, almonds, angelica, orris, cassia bark and juniper.

Other Brand:

Product Knowledge:

Product Wisdom:

Other Brand:

Product Knowledge:

Product Wisdom:

VODKA

Brand: Frïs

Product Knowledge: A premium import with a clean, pure taste.

Product Wisdom: Made with natural Scandinavian water and whole grain (not crushed), run through a three-step filtration process, then distilled six times to achieve the silkiness of the final product.

Brand: Absolut

Product Knowledge: A popular, smooth-tasting vodka known for its creative advertising campaigns.

Product Wisdom: Distilled from grain grown in southern Sweden in accordance with more than 400 years of tradition.

Brand: Stolichnaya

Product Knowledge: Distilled from rich grain and finished with pure glacial waters.

Product Wisdom: Imported from Russia, the birthplace of great vodkas.

Other Brand:

Product Knowledge:

Product Wisdom:

Other Brand:

Product Knowledge:

Product Wisdom:

RUM

Brand: Bacardi

Product Knowledge: Double-filtered through charcoal for smoothness and aged in charred white oak for character.

Product Wisdom: The world's first refined rum. A product of Puerto Rico.

Brand: Captain Morgan "Original Spiced Rum"

Product Knowledge: A golden Puerto Rican rum laced with spice.

Product Wisdom: Captain Morgan, famed buccaneer on the Spanish Main, favored a spicy life and a glass of his favorite rum.

Brand: Myers's "Original Dark"

Product Knowledge: A product of Jamaica with a rich, dark color and buttery flavor.

Product Wisdom: Distilled in the traditional pot still method, producing the rum's trademark characteristics.

Other Brand:

Product Knowledge:

Product Wisdom:

Other Brand:

Product Knowledge:

Product Wisdom:

TEQUILA

Brand: Sauza Conmemorativo

Product Knowledge: Distinguished by its deep, rich golden color and exceptional smoothness.

Product Wisdom: In the town of Tequila, Mexico, the patriarch of the Sauza family unlocked the secrets to making tequila in 1873.

Brand: Jose Cuervo Gold

Product Knowledge: Blended in large oak vats where the tequila rests against the wood, taking on a golden color and silky smooth flavor.

Product Wisdom: The world's oldest and largest tequila maker.

Brand: Patron

Product Knowledge: A premium tequila, smooth and crafted with great care.

Product Wisdom: Produced high in the mountains of Jalisco, Mexico, whose soil and climate are ideal for growing the Weaber Tequilana Blue Agave, from which comes the end product.

Other Brand:

Product Knowledge:

Product Wisdom:

Other Brand:

Product Knowledge:

Product Wisdom:

BRANDY AND COGNAC

Brand: Courvoisier V.S.

Product Knowledge: A cognac that stirs the senses, with a fruity, flowery aroma and pleasant character in the mouth.

Product Wisdom: During the aging process, the portion of cognac that evaporates into the air is called the "angel's share."

Brand: Grand Marnier

Product Knowledge: Very warm, amber-colored, made with exotic orange peels and fine old cognac brandy.

Product Wisdom: A bottle of Grand Marnier is sold every two seconds in the world.

Brand: Hennessy V.S.O.P. Privilege

Product Knowledge: A delicate, complex Cognac prized for its rich taste and distinctive bouquet.

Product Wisdom: First created for the British Royal Family in 1817.

Other Brand:

Product Knowledge:

Product Wisdom:

Other Brand:

Product Knowledge:

Product Wisdom:

CORDIALS AND LIQUEURS

Brand: Kahlúa

Product Knowledge: An exotic liqueur that mixes particularly well with after-dinner coffee drinks and desserts.

Product Wisdom: An import from Mexico whose sweetness has earned it the nickname "Brown Sugar."

Brand: Drambuie

Product Knowledge: Exceptionally smooth, yet brimming with a rich, complex and satisfying taste.

Product Wisdom: A Scottish liqueur made of fine-aged malt whiskies, honey and secret herbal essences.

Brand: Tuaca

Product Knowledge: A distinctive Italian liqueur, deliciously smooth, yet warming like a brandy.

Product Wisdom: Blended from fine-aged brandies and citrus fruits from Italy's Tuscan region. Recipe dates back to the Renaissance.

Other Brand:

Product Knowledge:

Product Wisdom:

Other Brand:

Product Knowledge:

Product Wisdom:

Less Is More

It's important to watch the amount of product wisdom you share with guests. You don't want to talk over their heads or put them to sleep with meaningless information. The idea is to make the experience fun and memorable.

It's your TURN

A well-dressed business person is interested in ordering a single-malt Scotch. What two brands could you recommend and how would you describe them? Write your response in the space below:

_____

_____

_____

_____

NOTE: *Be prepared to role play this scenario with your manager or trainer.*

Action STEP

There are many ways you can put to work what you've just learned about "product knowledge" and "product wisdom." But, for now, determine the three best ideas you picked up in this section and write them below:

The Three Best Ideas:

1. _____

2. _____

3. _____

At the end of *The Service That Sells! Workbook for Alcohol Beverage Service*, you'll be transferring these ideas to a Final Action Plan, which outlines your time line and game plan for improving your sales and service delivery with the strategies that work best for you.

Section Two: Caring Behavior

What's *Caring Behavior?* Many things, really. But all boiled down, it's making guests feel important.

Important enough to be:

- Acknowledged no later than a minute after they've been seated.
- Recognized if they're a regular customer.
- Taken care of with a smile, friendly eye contact and thoughtful guidance through the menu and the lineup of beer, wine and spirits.

Those are bare-minimum requirements — your day-in, day-out responsibilities in meeting guests' expectations. To *exceed* those expectations, however, you have to be ready, willing and able to do little something extras for guests. To pamper them in unexpected ways. To go beyond the routine.

That's what *Caring Behavior* is all about. And it's what separates the winners from the losers in the bar and restaurant business.

Little Something Extras

Guests essentially know what they want the minute they walk in the door. They want quality products at a fair price, delivered by an attentive server or bartender. Quality, value, service — that's what it takes for your operation to be successful.

Of the three, *service* is the chief ingredient to satisfaction. Quality and value mean zip if guests are subjected to inadequate service. In fact, it's not even enough to deliver adequate service. In the ultra-competitive bar and restaurant business, "good enough never is."

Performing "Little Something Extras" (LSE's) shows that you're willing to go beyond what's expected to make the most of the dining experience. Pulling out chairs for arriving guests is a good start. Then you can look for other moments during the meal to really shine.

The following exercise brings into focus the difference between adequate service and *Caring Behavior*. Consider the circumstances presented, then describe a possible adequate response you feel meets the minimum service requirements. Then describe a Little Something Extra you could use to comfort guests and make them feel important. As an example, the first one has been done for you.

Circumstance

You're busy serving a table when you see new guests arriving.

Your Adequate Response

Make an effort to get to them as fast as you can.

Your Little Something Extra

Make immediate eye contact, acknowledge their presence with a smile, warmly inform them that you'll be right there.

Circumstance

A guest claims you brought out the wrong drink, even though you're sure you placed the order correctly.

Your Adequate Response

_____

_____

Your Little Something Extra

_____

_____

Circumstance

A business person orders a vodka tonic made with a brand you don't carry.

Your Adequate Response

_____

_____

Your Little Something Extra

_____

_____

Circumstance

You're swamped and have been a little slow waiting on one of your customers.

Your Adequate Response

_____

_____

Your Little Something Extra

_____

_____

The importance of LSE's can't be stressed enough, whether you're waiting on tables or working behind the bar. As they say on Broadway, "start high and end high." Even if you're tied up serving others, try to make eye contact and smile at newly arriving guests, assuring them from the beginning that you're on the ball. At the end of the dining or drinking experience, thank guests for their business and invite them back for a return visit.

In between hello and good-bye, examples of _Caring Behavior_ abound. As you read through the following ideas, think about how you could apply them in your everyday work.

Personalize Your Service

Introduce yourself. Increasing the interaction between you and your guests enhances their experience and improves the odds that you'll get a higher tip.

Put it on PAPER What's another way you can build rapport with guests? Write your answer in the space below:

_____

_____

Watch Your Language

It's not just the words you use, but the manner in which you use them. Is the tone of your voice friendly? Are you sincere? Have you made eye contact? Guests appreciate servers and bartenders who care.

Talk the Talk

It's easy to strike up a conversation with guests when you use "Table Talk" to break the ice. There's plenty to say. Here are topics — positive hot buttons — that guests will usually warm to:

- Profession *("What line of work are you in?")*

- Appearance *("Great ballcap!")*

- Hometown *("Where did you grow up?")*

In the space below, name three more hot topics of discussion you can bring up with guests.

1. _____

2. _____

3. _____

Say You're Sorry

Poor service won't happen often — thanks in part to the effort you're putting into this workbook — but on the rare occasion it does, make amends by apologizing. Tell the guest what you plan to do to correct the problem.

Who knows? You might turn a bad situation into your selling advantage. Example: *"Sorry it took so long to get your glass of wine, Mr. Diaz. I'll be sure to deliver your second one as soon as you're ready."*

Stroke Your Customers

You don't need to go overboard, but a little flattery goes a long way *("Great tie, Mr. Jones!")*. Always mean what you say. Don't just say it to say it.

Pay Attention

A lot rides on presentation. Don't you just hate when your beer glass is warm or your water glass is spotted or your wine glass has a lipstick stain? Your customers hate it, too. If you wouldn't serve that beverage to yourself, don't serve it to your guests.

In the space below, write how you'd respond to a newly seated guest who complains that he's been waiting more than 10 minutes for service.

_____

_____

_____

NOTE: *Be prepared to role play this scenario with your manager or trainer.*

Add Some Flair

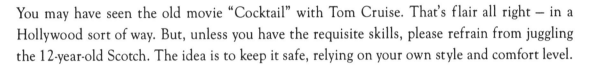

Another form of *Caring Behavior* can be described as "flair." In other words, the style with which you serve your guests.

You may have seen the old movie "Cocktail" with Tom Cruise. That's flair all right — in a Hollywood sort of way. But, unless you have the requisite skills, please refrain from juggling the 12-year-old Scotch. The idea is to keep it safe, relying on your own style and comfort level.

Attention, Bartenders: You can add flair to your service by simply having fun behind the bar. When pouring drinks, do you appear as if you're measuring nitroglycerin? Or do you exhibit a touch of rhythm?

Show extra-special care when handling bottles from the back bar or speed rack. Before pouring a drink at the bar, wipe down the bottle with a clean, dry towel as you turn the label toward the person who ordered that brand — in the same manner a server presents a bottle of wine. It adds value in the eyes of the guest and leaves a lasting impression.

Attention, Servers: You should get into the act, too. Show guests you're having fun — that there's a living, breathing person waiting on them, not some stiff on auto-pilot.

 A group of softball players have come into the bar to celebrate a recent victory. How could you play off their athletic prowess while adding flair to your work style? Write your response in the space below.

_____

_____

_____

NOTE: *Be prepared to role play this scenario with your manager or trainer.*

There's nothing wrong with playing it straight and being professional. But you just might find that adding flair to your service makes your work more enjoyable. Go about it in varying amounts, whatever you feel comfortable with. Keep in mind that some guests will be more receptive to your efforts than others. Use your best judgment.

 There are many ways you can put to work what you've just learned about *Caring Behavior*. But, for now, determine the three best ideas you picked up in this section and write them below.

The Three Best Ideas:

1. _____

2. _____

3. _____

At the end of *The Service That Sells! Workbook for Alcohol Beverage Service*, you'll be transferring these ideas to a Final Action Plan, which outlines your time line and game plan for improving your sales and service delivery with the strategies that work best for you.

Section Three: Precision Service

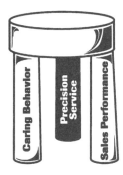

To be sure, guests appreciate *Caring Behavior*. But the warm-and-fuzziness will fade fast if there are breakdowns in the mechanics of the service delivery.

Did you get the order right? Was the drink garnished properly? Did the bartender follow the recipe? Were all the necessary condiments provided with the food or beverage?

These are all elements of *Precision Service*. Execute them seamlessly, and they'll more than likely go unnoticed by guests. Botch one or two, however, and the dining experience hangs in the balance.

Providing *Precision Service* is simply doing the job you were hired and trained to do. It's no problem, of course, when your section or bar is under control. The scene changes, however, when you get into "the weeds."

Stay Out of the Weeds

If you're like most servers or bartenders, you've spent some time in "the weeds" — that unique piece of restaurant real estate where you're out of control, swamped, sweating, losing it, freaking out, and ready to find a *real* job.

It's a common nightmare. But you can't wake up from this one. Who suffers? Everyone does. Guests have to interact with flipped-out servers, who often blame customers for their lack of patience. The end result is bad service, low sales and lackluster repeat business.

It's order-takers — not salespeople — who get into trouble. Here's why:

- They waited for the guest to decide what's good without offering any guidance or suggestions.
- They didn't have enough product knowledge to answer a question about a particular item.
- They forgot to bring out something that was supposed to accompany the order.

What's the secret to staying out of the weeds and in the money? O.A.P.A. — Observe, Anticipate, Prioritize, Act.

Observe. Keep an eye on your section or bar. See who needs what. Scan the faces of your guests. Do they need anything?

Anticipate. When approaching newly seated guests, anticipate their needs by asking: *"Can I get you something from the bar? A glass of wine, cocktail, beer. We're featuring Sutter Home and Clos Du Bois wines by the glass."* Try to make suggestions before the guest has to ask.

Prioritize. Which guests need your attention first? Second? Third? Always acknowledge new-comers first. They can be anxious. Other priorities include guests who have a problem with their food or beverage, guests who just received their food or beverage (try to check back after they've had two bites or two sips), and guests who are ready to pay.

Act. Don't just re-act. Control your section before it controls you. How? Through suggestive selling. The funny thing about the restaurant business is that to stay out of the weeds you can never be in the present. You have to focus on what you have to do next.

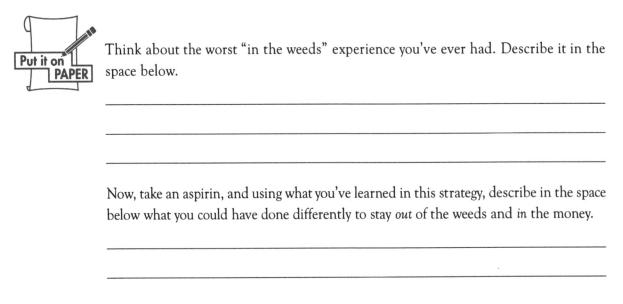

Think about the worst "in the weeds" experience you've ever had. Describe it in the space below.

_____

_____

_____

Now, take an aspirin, and using what you've learned in this strategy, describe in the space below what you could have done differently to stay *out* of the weeds and *in* the money.

_____

_____

_____

Drive I-135

A lot of *Precision Service* is about timing — bringing guests what they want ... *when* they want it. But even the best servers can get bogged down, especially when they have three tables full and two more have just been seated.

Not to worry. There's help up ahead. It's called I-135, a highway that leads to better service and higher sales. Here's what it means:

I: Immediately acknowledge your guests. Say it with a smile even if you're busy. Drop a cocktail napkin or coaster on the table in front of them and say, "I'll be right with you." Remember these words: "Grace under pressure."

1: Try to take the initial beverage order within one minute. Sixty seconds doesn't sound like a long time, does it? But to the guest a minute may seem like an eternity.

3: Deliver the beverage and suggest an appetizer within three minutes.

5: Check back for drink refills or the appetizer sale within five minutes.

Put it on PAPER Let's make sure you've got the I-135 steps down. Writing them below will help you remember them.

I: _____

1: _____

3: _____

5: _____

Did you get them all right? Then let's move on to...

The Perfect Pour

Attention, Bartenders: You play a key role in making sure the beer you serve turns out to be the beer guests expect. The perfect pour begins with a "beer clean" glass — one thoroughly washed and rinsed, then stored upside-down on a raised mat that allows air to circulate. Don't put the glasses upside-down on a towel to dry. It contaminates the end product. And never, ever serve beer in a warm glass, no matter how clean it is.

Now you're ready to pour. Grab the tap handle at the *base*, opening the faucet all the way in a quick, smooth motion. Pulling from the top starts the flow too slowly, which causes excessive foam. In the beginning, tilt the glass at a 45-degree angle, then straighten as you pour, being careful not to overfill and shooting for a one-inch collar of foam.

Why a foam head? Because it produces a better-tasting and better-looking product. A beer with little or no foam seems flat and retains CO_2 gas, which guests swallow. As a result, they get filled up faster, and your operation sells less beer.

A proper foam head amounts to nothing, however, if it has disappeared by the time the beer reaches the guest. Bartenders should always prepare wine and mixed drinks before the beer portion of the order. Servers, meanwhile, should be staged nearby, ready to deliver the goods while they're still good.

Put it on PAPER

In the spaces below, write three "do's" when it comes to pouring a perfect beer and three "don'ts." Feel free to use the tips previously mentioned or, better yet, include ones based on your own experience or procedures in your operation.

Do's:

1. _____

2. _____

3. _____

Don'ts:

1. _____

2. _____

3. _____

Opening Wine

Attention, Servers: You should carry a wine opener with you at all times. First of all, it's tough to open a bottle without one. Second, if you can operate a corkscrew with confidence, you'll be well on your way to wine-selling success.

Here's a step-by-step guide to opening, presenting and pouring wine:

- With the label facing toward the host (the person who placed the order), present the wine and repeat its name: *"Your Sutter Home Merlot..."*

- With the knife part of the corkscrew, cut just below the lip of the bottle to remove the foil. Put the foil in your apron, not on the table or bar.

- Wipe the top of the bottle with a napkin.

- Place the point of the corkscrew in the middle of the cork and turn firmly. Try to keep the point in the middle of the cork and apply more pressure as you turn.

- After three or four turns, take the fulcrum of the corkscrew and latch it to the lip of the bottle.

- Pull up slowly, until the cork releases from the bottle.

- Remove the cork from the corkscrew and place it in front of the host.

- Wipe off the top of the bottle again.

- Hold the bottle with the label facing toward your guests and pour a sample of wine into the host's glass.

- After the host approves the wine, pour it clockwise around the table to women first, men second and the host last. Pour each glass about two-thirds full, taking care that you don't touch the rim of the glass with the bottle.

- To avoid dripping wine on a guest or on the table, twist and pull the bottle up in one smooth motion as you finish pouring.

- For parties of five or more, use good judgment when pouring to make sure everyone gets some wine. You may have to fill the glasses less than two-thirds full to accommodate each guest. If you're unsure how far the bottle will go, it's better to pour less than too much. The best approach of all, however, is to suggest two bottles of wine at the start. Then you'll have plenty to go around.

- After pouring the wine, place red wines on the table in front of the host. White wine bottles should be placed in a ceramic or metal chiller.

Review the previous wine-opening steps, paying particular attention to any techniques you're not currently doing. Then, before the start of an upcoming shift, go to the bartender and offer to open a bottle of the house wine. Open it the same precise way you'd do it in front of guests. Practice makes perfect.

NOTE: *Be prepared to open a bottle in front of your manager or trainer.*

That's the Spirit

When serving cocktails, presentation is key. Guests want to feel like they're getting something out of the ordinary, especially if they've ordered a premium or super-premium pour. They don't want to see, for example, a brown, dried-out lemon wedge adorning their Frïs and Tonic.

A simple rotation system will help keep fresh fruit fresh. Remember: "First in, first out. Last in, last out." And, if it's your job, be sure to cover cut fruit thoroughly at closing time. A little prevention goes a long way.

For servers, it's bad form — as well as unsanitary — to present drink orders after you've carried them by the rim of the glass. Instead, grab hold at the base or stem. You shouldn't be touching where guests will be sipping.

At the point you present the drink, make it a habit to repeat the brand name. Don't say: *"Here's your gin Martini."* Do say: *"Here's your Beefeater Martini."*

Repeating the brand enhances guests' perception of quality and shows that you know what *Precision Service* is all about.

There are many ways you can put to work what you've just learned about *Precision Service*. But, for now, determine the three best ideas you picked up in this section and write them below.

The Three Best Ideas:

1. _____

2. _____

3. _____

At the end of *The Service That Sells! Workbook for Alcohol Beverage Service*, you'll be transferring these ideas to a Final Action Plan, which outlines your time line and game plan for improving your sales and service delivery with the strategies that work best for you.

Section Four: Sales Performance

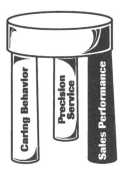

To excel at selling alcohol beverages, it's wise to keep up with the trends. The business, for instance, has seen a re-emergence of what was hip in the 1950s — minus some of the excess. The "One Martini Lunch," for example, has taken the place of its two-round predecessor.

Consumers today want to live a little and reward themselves for the long hours they put in at work. Favoring quality over quantity, they've developed a tendency to splurge, ordering more and more hand-crafted beers, high-end wines by the glass, and premium spirits.

Why settle for a run-of-the-mill Scotch when guests could savor a Glendronach? The beer list these days rivals the wine list in magnitude.

You'll have to do your homework in order to keep pace with guests' widening brand awareness. If you remain on top of things, the stage will be set to sell more of what guests are asking for.

Prop Up Your Sales

You can sell more beer, wine and spirits when you make use of the sales props at your disposal. Tap handles, beer and wine lists, reader boards, table tents — all can help visually reinforce what you're recommending.

Just direct the guest's attention to one of your sales props as you smile, then deliver your dialogue:

"This Samuel Adams Boston Lager is my favorite beer on tap right now (pointing to a branded coaster)."

"Those guests (calling attention to the wine bottle on an adjacent table) are enjoying the Sutter Home Cabernet Sauvignon. It would go perfectly with your Prime Rib."

"We're featuring top-shelf Margaritas tonight made with Sauza Conmemorativo (pointing to a table tent). Anyone interested?"

List three sales props you can use to sell more beer, wine or spirits on your very next shift:

_____

_____

_____

Recommend the Larger Size

This is a simple but powerful sales strategy, particularly effective when selling beer.

If a guest orders something on draft, *always* say "Large?" as you nod your head up and down.

If a guest orders any other beverage that comes in different sizes, *always* say "Large?" as you nod your head up and down.

Recommending the large size gives guests a better value, earns you more tips and can save you steps. How many times has a customer ordered a small beverage, gulped it down, then sent you off running for another one, usually another small? Save yourself the wear and tear. Think big.

While you're at it, think "pitcher" if two or more guests are ordering the same brand. The most effective recommendations highlight the value: *"How about a pitcher, since you're both drinking Coors Light? You end up getting an extra glass for free."*

Break It Down

Sometimes guests can't seem to decide what they want, and they'll look to you for help. You'll seem inept if you're at a loss for words. Your sales will suffer, too. An effective way to guide the indecisive is to narrow down their preferences.

When recommending beer, try:

> *"What type of beer do you like – light, dark or middle of the road?"*

> Then ask: *"Domestic, imported or microbrew?"*

We're talking Customer Service 101 here – the same way a retail associate might start the sales process for a pair of men's shoes by asking, "Are you looking for black shoes or brown? Ties or loafers?"

A couple of happy hour guests seem overwhelmed with the number of beers available. How would you help them decide what to get? Write what you'd say in the space below.

_____

_____

_____

NOTE: *Be prepared to role play this scenario with your manager or trainer.*

Get to the Point

A lot of times guests come in predisposed to order beer, wine or spirits. You don't need to waste time spouting long-winded sales dialogue and an endless string of descriptive adjectives. Instead, use hip, to-the-point dialogue — Pinpoint Dialogue — to make the sale.

Example:

> *Server:* "Beers, guys?"
>
> *Guest:* "What's good?"
>
> *Server:* "I like the Full Sail Amber Ale or the Samuel Adams Boston Lager. Which sounds best?"
>
> *Guest:* "The second one."

When using Pinpoint Dialogue, lead with any beverage specials your bar or restaurant is running. If you suggest and sell something more expensive right off the bat, guests might feel ripped off upon the discovery that they could have enjoyed something else at a discounted price.

Assume the Sale

If you want to increase the persuasiveness of your recommendations, try not to ask questions that can be easily dismissed with a "yes" or "no" response. Instead, assume that you're going to make the sale.

> *Wrong way:* "Would you care for a Martini or something?"
>
> *Right way:* "Our Martinis are the best in town. We carry a wide variety of gins and vodkas, but if you want something really smooth, I'd recommend either Beefeater gin or Frïs vodka. Which would you prefer?"

Can you hear the difference? Be pleasant, never pushy, when attempting this advanced selling strategy. And always punctuate your recommendations with a warm smile.

Circle the dialogue that best illustrates "assuming the sale:"

A: *"Would you care for some wine with your steaks this evening?"*

B: *"You know what would go really well with your steaks is a Sutter Home Cabernet Sauvignon or perhaps a Robert Mondavi Cabernet Sauvignon. Which sounds better to you?*

Five Times To Sell Wine

When guests don't take the initiative to order wine on their own, you have to be proactive. Knowing when to bring up the idea and when to close in on the sale can mean the difference between getting a "yes" or a "no, thanks."

When Seating Guests. As guests take their seats, the host or hostess should present the wine list, pointing out specials and specific offerings. When the server visits the table a minute later, the seed for the wine sale will have been planted, increasing the likelihood of a taker.

What could a host or hostess say to plant the seed for a wine sale? Write the dialogue in the space below:

_____

_____

_____

When Greeting Guests. At the initial-greeting stage, servers should pick up where the host or hostess left off, suggesting a premium varietal either by the glass or bottle. A powerful way to proceed is to mention wine in general at first, then get more specific at the end of your dialogue. Example:

"May I start you off with something from the bar – a glass of wine, a beer, a cocktail? Tonight we're featuring Clos Du Bois Chardonnay by the glass and bottle."

Take notice of how the recommendation starts off in simple terms — "a glass of wine" — then goes into more detail — "we're featuring Clos Du Bois Chardonnay." This approach gets results because guests tend to remember the first and last things you say.

Suggesting wine by the glass makes sense when guests can't agree on a particular wine, or when they want to sample a selection or two before settling on a bottle, or when they want to start with, say, a Chardonnay, then switch to a Cabernet with the meal.

How would you suggest a bottle of wine to a four-top, using the strategy of saying it first and last? Write the dialogue in the space below.

_____

_____

_____

If guests are considering wine by the glass, and they're gravitating toward the same one, that's your cue to suggest sharing a bottle. Example:

> *"Since you're both having the same wine, you might want to consider a bottle. You'll each get about two glasses and you'll save some money."*

Upgrading the order will save you steps. It's so much easier and less time consuming to pour from a bottle that's already on the table than to chase down multiple wines by the glass. Underscoring the value of the upgrade is always a good idea.

When Checking Back with Guests. Just because wine has been ordered doesn't mean the selling stops. When checking back on food quality or seeing to beverage refills, always fill the glasses of those drinking wine. When the bottle runs dry, suggest another one.

What would you say to guests to sell the second bottle? Write the dialogue in the space below.

_____

_____

_____

Short-and-sweet tends to be the most effective second-bottle dialogue. *"How about another bottle?"* might be just the ticket.

When Shortening the Wait. Another wine-selling opportunity exists between the delivery of the soup or salad and the entree. This period, the longest delay diners face, is the perfect time to suggest wine by the glass, split or bottle, making sure you know your guests' preferences. Ask these three questions to find out:

> *"Have you had a chance to look over our wine list? I'd be happy to help you with any questions you have."*

> *"Do you prefer red or white?"*

> *"Sweet or dry?"*

With this line of questioning, you can guide your guests and narrow down the choices. Selling a second bottle of wine in this instance is a snap. As you pour the last of the wine, slowly nod your head up and down in an affirmative action and ask:

"Would you like to enjoy another bottle with your entrees?"

Put it on PAPER In the space below, write three questions you could use to narrow down a guest's wine selection.

1. _____

2. _____

3. _____

Did you ask what the guest was planning to eat? Whether he or she wanted a red or white wine? Sweet or dry? Once you're in position to offer guidance, you can let your product wisdom shine, impressing guests and tipping the tips scale in your favor.

Last But Not Least. The last time to suggest and sell wine is at the end of the meal. Ports, for example, complement desserts containing nuts. Sparking wines go well with fresh-fruit selections. Dry cabernets bring out the flavor in chocolate-based desserts.

With so many ways to suggest and sell wine, success is all but guaranteed — especially if you keep at it, recommending wine whenever the opportunity presents itself. Sure, you'll win some and you'll lose some. But the greater your enthusiasm, the higher your winning percentage will be.

Catch the Spirit

The practice of upgrading well orders to call brands should be a reflex action for you. Always suggest your best when serving guests. They'll get a better tasting drink. You'll earn a better tip.

That doesn't mean to go over the top, trying to push the most expensive stuff. It does mean taking "baby steps," asking targeted questions to uncover what guests like and what they need to enhance their dining or drinking experience. Armed with that essential information, you can move guests up the ladder, one rung at a time.

When a guest orders a mixed drink, don't automatically settle for the house pour. Suggest an upgrade to a premium brand. Example:

Guest: "I'll have a Manhattan."

Server: *"Would you like to try a Canadian Club Manhattan? It's a house favorite."*

Did you notice the word "try" in the dialogue? It lets guests know that the premium pour will cost a little extra, but it'll make the drink taste much better.

It's your TURN A guest asks for a dirty Martini up. In the space below, write what you'd say to suggest an upgrade.

_____

_____

_____

NOTE: *Be prepared to role play this scenario with your manager or trainer.*

When suggesting your best, you can reverse your suggestive-selling strategy but achieve the same positive results. Simply ask guests if *they* have a favorite. If someone wants a whiskey and water, you might ask: *"Do you have a favorite whiskey that you prefer?"*

And if you want to just about guarantee the sale, say it this way: *"Do you prefer a specific whiskey? We feature Maker's Mark!"*

Go for Two

Selling the first drink to a guest gets the ball rolling, but selling the second is what separates the pros from the one-shot wonders. Besides, going for two is the easiest way to double your sales.

A mistake servers and bartenders often make is to wait until guests have finished drink No. 1 before suggesting No. 2. You'll be much more successful and perceived to be much more attentive if you "overlap" your timing, suggesting the second round at the point the drink is one-half to two-thirds gone. By the time guests have finished their first, they'll be happy to see their second arrive.

When delivering your second-round suggestions, avoid using sales dialogue that makes the order seem excessive. Try the word "fresh:"

> *"How about a fresh Martini?"*

Sounds inviting, doesn't it?

It's your TURN

You notice one of your guests is halfway through his Margarita. What would you say to sell him a second round? Write your response in the space below.

_____

_____

_____

NOTE: *Be prepared to role play this scenario with your manager or trainer.*

The Parade

Whenever you're delivering a flashy specialty drink or, say, a glamorous Martini, carry it through the dining room at about guests' eye level. By the time you reach the final destination, you'll have tempted a number of onlookers along the way.

Put it on PAPER

In the space below, write three specialty drinks you could parade through the dining room to boost sales.

1. _____

2. _____

3. _____

Action STEP

There are many ways you can put to work what you've just learned about *Sales Performance*. But, for now, determine the three best ideas you picked up in this section and write them below.

The Three Best Ideas:

1. _____

2. _____

3. _____

At the end of *The Service That Sells! Workbook for Alcohol Beverage Service*, you'll be transferring these ideas to a Final Action Plan, which outlines your time line and game plan for improving your sales and service delivery with the strategies that work best for you.

In fact, it starts on the next page.

Final Action Plan

The last task in *Work Smarter, Not Harder! The Service That Sells! Workbook for Alcohol Beverage Service* is to figure out how you're going to do what you've just learned to do. The best advice? Just do it.

In the Final Action Plan starting below and continuing on the next three pages, transfer the "Action Steps" you identified at the end of each section — pages 26, 32, 38, 46. You should have 12 total.

Write the "Start Date" you plan to implement each Action Step. A month later return to this Final Action Plan and describe the "30-Day Results" you've experienced. We're sure you'll be pleasantly surprised.

Section One: Product Knowledge

[1] Action Step:

Start Date:

30-Day Results:

[2] Action Step:

Start Date:

30-Day Results:

[3] Action Step:

Start Date:

30-Day Results:

Section Two: Caring Behavior

4   Action Step:

Start Date:

30-Day Results:

5   Action Step:

Start Date:

30-Day Results:

6   Action Step:

Start Date:

30-Day Results:

Section Three: Precision Service

7   Action Step:

       Start Date:

       30-Day Results:

8   Action Step:

       Start Date:

       30-Day Results:

9   Action Step:

       Start Date:

       30-Day Results:

Section Four: Sales Performance

10   Action Step:

        Start Date:

        30-Day Results:

11   Action Step:

        Start Date:

        30-Day Results:

12   Action Step:

        Start Date:

        30-Day Results:

And One Last Thing...

Now that you've completed *Work Smarter, Not Harder! The Service That Sells! Workbook for Alcohol Beverage Service*, it's up to you to put the ideas to work. You have everything to gain — higher sales, bigger tips, better service — and nothing to lose.

Here's how to maximize your results:

- Keep your Final Action Plan where you can refer to it. Make a commitment to put the ideas to use.
- Keep track of how much your tips increase after reading the workbook.
- Re-read the workbook from time to time. You may pick up on something you missed the first time around.

Pencom International Products ... to build your bottom line.

VIDEOS

Service That Sells!
The Art of Profitable Hospitality

The 12 Moments of Truth that made *Service That Sells!* an international success have been updated in this new release of our best-selling video. *Caring Behavior, Precision Service* and *Sales Performance* — the three legs of *Service That Sells!* — will show your staff how to manage the guest experience effectively from start to finish. *Full Service version* **$99**; *Family Dining version* **$99**

CheckBusters: The Art of Smart Selling

Raise check averages a minimum of 25 cents per person — or your money back. Fun and fast-paced, *CheckBusters* is loaded with tips and techniques that promote sales while enhancing how guests perceive the quality of service your staff provides. **$149**

CheckBusters Workbooks. Ideal for a comprehensive program and training retention. **25 for $69.95; 50 for $99.95**

Heads Up! Tapping into Craft Beer

More fun than a hoppy pilsner, *Heads Up!* demystifies the endless varieties of craft beer on the market, giving bartenders and servers the knowledge and brewing background they need to sell and serve with the best. **$69**

Pour on the Profits

Teach your staff how to maximize sales and service potential at the bar using "table talk" to break down conversational barriers and "product wisdom" to put guests in a buying mood. **$99**

The "Sell More" Series

Focus your sales training with the "Sell More" series. Perfect for viewing at pre-shift meetings.

Sell More Beer — **$69**

Sell More Wine — **$69**

Sell More Appetizers — **$69**

Sell More Desserts — **$69**

Uncommon Grounds:
Cashing in on the Coffee Craze

Educate servers in the art of selling and serving specialty coffees. *Uncommon Grounds* explores the ins and outs of preparation, product knowledge and promoting add-ons. **$69**

NEWSLETTER

The Service That Sells! Newsletter

Get the edge on your competition for a quarter a day. Service, sales, cost control, leadership, marketing — the management tool you need to run a profitable operation. One-year subscription **$99**, two-year subscription **$149**. Canada **$139** per year. International **$169** per year. Multiple subscription rates available.

BOOKS

Service That Sells!
The Art of Profitable Hospitality

This is it. The best-selling book in foodservice history. More than 300,000 sold. An indispensable resource for restaurant owners, operators and managers committed to profitable hospitality and getting the most out of their employees. *English* or *Spanish* **$16.95**

Quick Service That Sells!

The profit-building approach that made *STS! The Book* a best-seller is adapted to quick service in this must-have resource. Speed, accuracy, quality, value, consistency, service, atmosphere, personalization – *Quick Service That Sells!* shows QSR operators how to excel in these critical moments of truth. **$16.95**

Turn the Tables on Turnover: 52 Ways To Find, Hire and Keep the Best Hospitality Employees

Lower your turnover by bringing on the right employees and giving them plenty of reasons to stay. **$19.95**

Playing Games at Work: 52 Best Incentives, Contests and Rewards

Boost staff morale and productivity with these fun, manageable and results-oriented incentive programs, contributed by readers of the *Service That Sells! Newsletter.* **$19.95**

Pump Up Your Profits: 52 Cost-Saving Ideas To Build Your Bottom Line

Save a bundle in lost revenue this year with tried-and-true measures to widen your profit margins and narrow your wasteful practices. **$19.95**

Pour It On: 52 Ways To Maximize Bar Sales

Make the most of your adult-beverage sales and service with this invaluable behind-the-bar tool. **$19.95**

All for One: 52 Ways To Build a Winning Team

Discover how to choose the right team players, develop team-building skills and unite the entire staff with these strategies. **$19.95**

www.pencominternational.com

Get connected

The Pencom International website is more than a company snapshot. It's a meeting of the minds, where foodservice operators and manufacturers can:

- Interact in a virtual exchange of ideas
- Take part in hot-button industry polls
- Get Real World Training Solutions

All at the click of a mouse.

Updated weekly, the website delivers free sample pages of the *Service That Sells!* Newsletter, restaurant-tested productivity tools and techniques, exclusive offers for visitors, and links to many other important foodservice sites.

Hop online. Every product in this listing — and many more — can be ordered off the Pencom International Website through a secure line. Save time when you know what you want. Get the solutions you need – when you need them. Visit us today at **www.pencominternational.com.**